Alfred's
Essentials of MUSIC Theory

TEACHER'S ACTIV

30 Reproducible Activities, Plus 6 Tests

ANDREW SURMANI • KAREN FARNUM SURMANI • MORTON MANUS

Foreword

Alfred's Essentials of Music Theory, in books and software, has quickly become one of the most widely used theory courses. In order for students to learn new concepts thoroughly, however, it is necessary to repeat and reinforce those concepts in unique ways. The reproducible pages of Activities and Tests included in *Teacher's Activity Kit*, Book 1 will help every student become more familiar with concepts introduced in Book 1 of the *Alfred's Essentials of Music Theory* course.

Though correlated with *Alfred's Essentials of Music Theory*, Book 1, the materials in this kit may also be used to advantage with any theory text.

Unique features of *Teacher's Activity Kit*, Book 1:

Activities
There are five Activities in each of the six Units, which correlate specifically to the six Units in Book 1 of *Alfred's Essentials of Music Theory*. The wide variety of Activities includes Music Crossword Puzzles, Note Naming, Matching Games, Musical Math, Word Scrambles, Word Searches, and others for a total of 30 Activities in all.

Tests
There is one Test per Unit that covers all the theory concepts introduced in that Unit.

Scorekeeping
Each reproducible page includes scoring boxes to help the instructor grade the page.

Record Keeping
There is one reproducible Grade Form page, with a grid to keep track of the students' scores for every page in the Kit.

Answer Key
Answers for every Activity and Test page are included in a reduced size to assist in the grading process.

The *Teacher's Activity Kit* is the perfect "teacher saver" for days when a substitute is required—activities can be offered easily and as needed.

Thanks to:
Bruce Goldes,
Matt McKagan
and Kate Westin

Alfred Publishing Co., Inc.
16320 Roscoe Blvd., Suite 100
P.O. Box 10003
Van Nuys, CA 91410-0003
alfred.com

Alfred

Copyright © MM by Alfred Publishing Co., Inc.
All rights reserved.   Printed in USA.
ISBN-10: 0-7390-0873-0
ISBN-13: 978-0-7390-0873-7

How to Use This Kit

Page Numbering

Each page in *Teacher's Activity Kit*, Book 1 is labeled at the top with a Unit number, Activity number, and a correlating page reference.

- The Unit number tells which Unit of *Alfred's Essentials of Music Theory*, Book 1 contains the topic the Activity reinforces.
- The Activity number indicates the sequence of Activities within each Unit.
- The specific page in *Alfred's Essentials of Music Theory*, Book 1 with which the Activity may be assigned is given at the upper right-hand corner of each sheet. When more than one Activity correlates to the same page in the *Essentials of Music Theory* text book, the Activities may be assigned in any order.
- There is also a space at the top of each page for the student to write his or her name and class.

Scorekeeping

Each Activity and Test page indicates how points are to be scored so that the page may be graded. The point system to be used is determined by the type of exercise(s) on the page. Every page has a three-part box at the bottom where the scores and total grade for that page is recorded.

1. On a page where each correct answer earns the same number of points, the three-part box is used as follows:

   - The bottom part of the box has two numbers. The first number indicates how many points are to be earned for each correct answer. The second number is the total number of points that may be earned for the entire page (this will always total 100).
   - The middle part of the box is where the number of points actually earned is written.
   - The top part of the box is for you to write your grade for that page.

2. When a page contains different exercises with varying point amounts, a box divided into halves will appear to the right of each exercise:

   - The first number in the bottom half of the box indicates the number of points to score for each individual correct answer within the exercise.

- The second number in the bottom half of the box is the total amount of points that can be earned for correctly answering all the items in that exercise. If a box has only one number in the bottom half of the box, it indicates a flat score for that exercise.
- The top half of the box is for you to record the number of points actually earned for the exercise.

Record Keeping

At the back of the Kit (page 48) is a record-keeping form for listing students and all their grades, organized by Unit.

Topics Covered in Each Unit

Unit 1   *page 3*
Staff, notes and pitches
Treble and bass clefs and staffs
Grand staff and ledger lines

Unit 2   *page 9*
Note values
Measure, barline and double bar
$\frac{4}{4}$ time and note values
Whole, half and quarter rests

Unit 3   *page 15*
$\frac{2}{4}$ and $\frac{3}{4}$ time
Dotted half note
Ties and slurs

Unit 4   *page 21*
Repeat sign, 1st and 2nd endings
Eighth notes and rests
Dotted quarter note

Unit 5   *page 27*
Dynamic signs, tempo marks
Articulation
D.C., D.S., Coda, Fine

Unit 6   *page 33*
Flats, sharps and naturals
Whole and half steps
Enharmonic notes

Answer Keys   *page 39*

Unit 1 ACTIVITY 1 Name/Class_____

Dinner for Two Spell words by writing the note names to complete the sentences below.

One day, ____ ____ ____ met her old friend ____ ____ at a ____ ____ ____

for dinner. ____ hostess led them through the ____ ____ ____ ____ ____ ____ curtain to

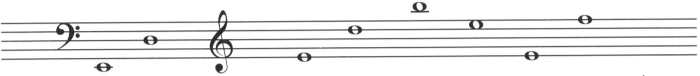

their table. ____ ____ ordered the corn____ ____ ____ ____ ____ and

____ ____ ____ ____ ____ ____ while ____ ____ ____ ordered an ____ ____ ____ salad sandwich

and lemon____ ____ ____ . They ate and chatted about musical i____ ____ ____ s and their

favorite composers. Finally, ____ ____ ____ called for a doggy ____ ____ ____ .

The waiter ____ ____ ____ ____ ____ up their ____ ____ ____ and brought it to the table.

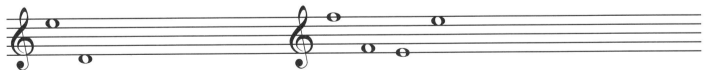

____ ____ said, "I've decided to order co ____ ____ ____ ____ ."

"I'll have some, too," said ____ ____ ____ ,"but make mine ____ ____ ____ ____ ____ ."

5*100	

*5 points for
each group

Unit 1 ACTIVITY 2 Name/Class_____

Staff and Keyboard Note Naming
Write the names of the given notes below the staff and on the keyboard above. In the box to the right of each staff, indicate the letter that is repeated.

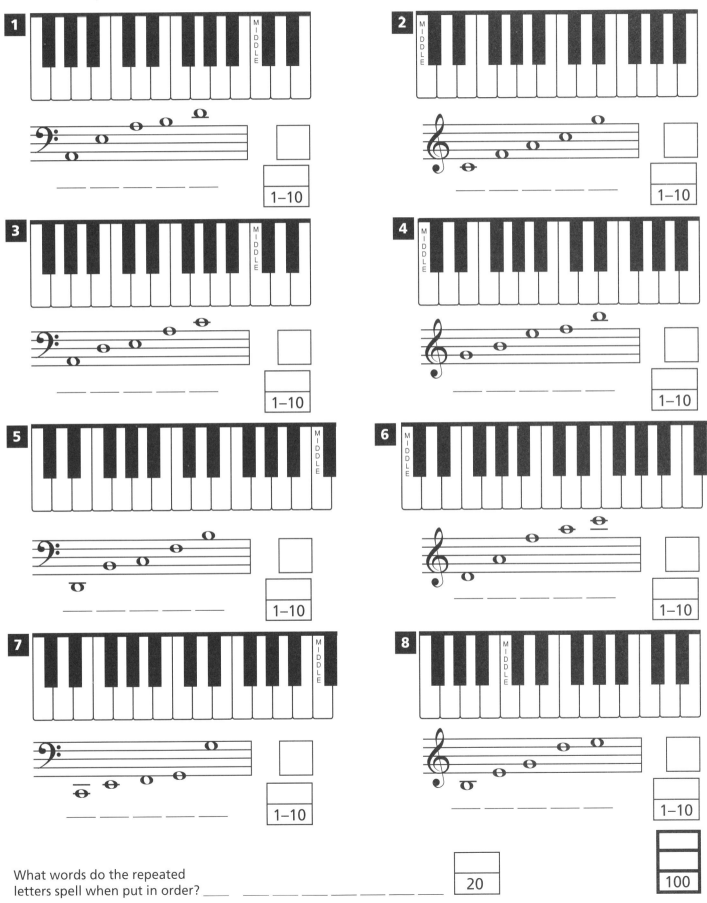

What words do the repeated letters spell when put in order? ____ ____ ____ ____ ____ ____ ____

4

Unit 1 ACTIVITY 3 Name/Class_____
Note Naming

1 Write the letter names of these notes from the treble staff.

[1–16]

2 Write the letter names of these notes from the bass staff.

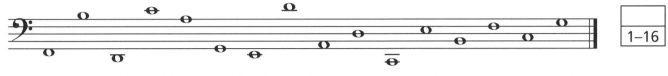

[1–16]

3 Draw a treble clef. Draw the indicated notes in two places on the staff.
Use ledger lines as needed.

[2–12]

A   F   B   G   C   E   D

4 Draw a bass clef. Draw the indicated notes in two different places on the staff.
Use ledger lines as needed.

[2–12]

E   B   G   D   A   C   F

5 Complete the grand staff by drawing the treble and bass clefs, and the connecting brace
and line. Draw the indicated notes in four different places on the grand staff.

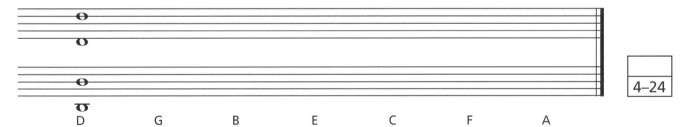

[4–24]

D   G   B   E   C   F   A

6 For each line, circle the measure that has a note named differently from the others.

[4–12]

Circle each measure that does not have three notes with the same letter name.

7

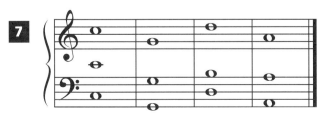

[4–8]

[ ]

[100]

Unit 1 ACTIVITY 4   Name/Class_____

Word Search

Find the words from the list below and circle them in the puzzle.
Words may appear forward, backward, up, down or diagonally, and may overlap.

S	F	B	S	W	H	P	L	I	N	E	S	W	W	T
L	E	C	A	F	D	T	M	W	G	O	R	C	W	Q
I	L	N	C	D	G	M	U	N	D	C	T	A	R	Z
U	C	L	I	M	S	N	S	U	G	C	L	E	F	A
R	E	W	O	L	O	Y	I	U	E	B	H	F	S	P
F	L	H	W	B	R	K	C	F	W	G	A	J	I	J
X	B	Y	T	O	M	E	W	D	I	T	Y	T	X	P
F	E	W	E	R	L	Y	G	H	S	E	C	A	P	S
C	R	H	E	D	X	B	S	D	X	H	J	E	S	O
A	T	E	D	T	Q	O	N	F	E	C	W	F	P	O
P	G	I	W	Y	B	A	S	S	C	L	E	F	F	A
S	M	A	M	Z	R	R	O	Z	A	S	K	A	V	W
M	B	E	I	G	P	D	V	P	R	Q	K	T	A	G
R	E	W	O	T	B	Z	J	J	B	D	W	S	O	P

Bass clef	Keyboard	Pitches
Brace	Ledger lines	Spaces
F clef	Lines	Staff
FACE	Lower	Symbol
G clef	Middle C	Theory
Grand staff	Music	Treble clef
Higher	Notes	

5–100

6

Unit 1 ACTIVITY 5 Name/Class_____

Music Crossword Puzzle

ACROSS	
1. The bass and treble staffs connected by a brace and barline (2 words)	13. A sign that helps organize the staff so notes can be easily read
3. Clef used for notes in the lower pitch ranges	14. Good Boys Do Fine _____ (bass staff line notes)
6. Another name for the musical sounds represented by notes	16. The oval-shaped symbols placed on the staff to represent musical sounds
8. The staff on which F is the fourth line (2 words)	18. What the treble staff space notes spell
10. Another name for the bass clef (2 words)	19. All _____ Eat Grass (bass staff space notes)
11. Lines that extend the lower and upper ranges of a staff (2 words)	20. Line number 5 of the staff is the _____ line.

DOWN	
2. The staff on which G is the second line (2 words)	15. Is space number 1 the *highest* or *lowest* space of the staff?
4. The five lines and four spaces upon which music is written	17. Every _____ Boy Does Fine (treble staff line notes)
5. The "C" nearest the center of a piano keyboard (2 words)	
7. Music notes are named after the first _____ letters of the alphabet.	
9. Clef used for notes in the higher pitch ranges	
12. Another name for the treble clef (2 words)	

7

5–100

Unit 1 TEST   Name/Class_____

1 The G clef is also known as the_____clef.   The F clef is also known as the_____clef.

| 1–2 |

2 Draw the treble clef and write the letter names of the notes.

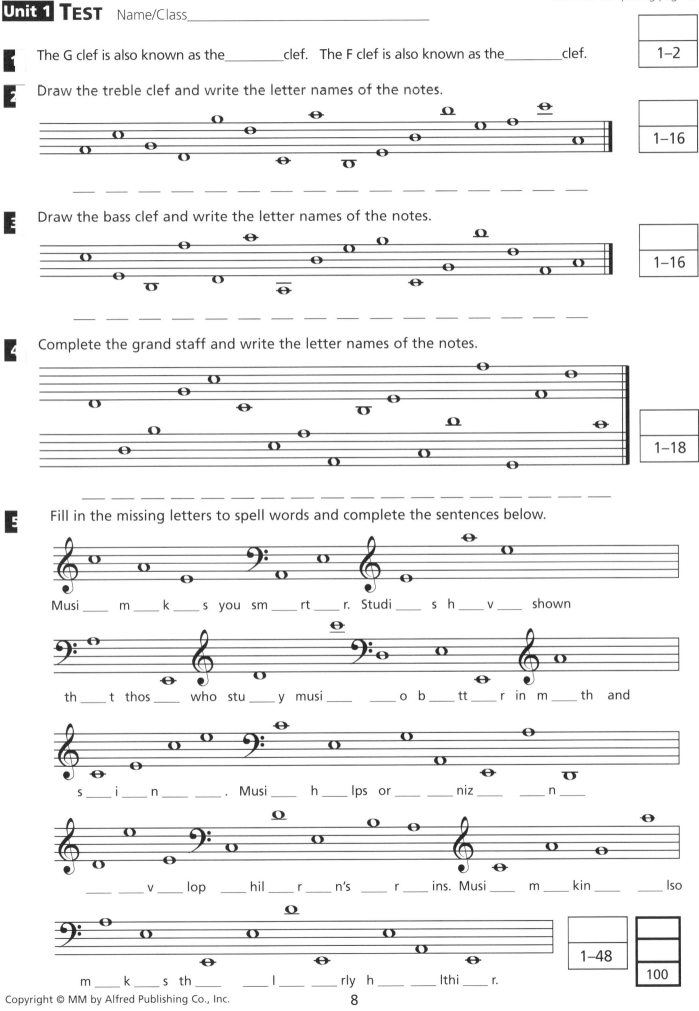

| 1–16 |

3 Draw the bass clef and write the letter names of the notes.

| 1–16 |

4 Complete the grand staff and write the letter names of the notes.

| 1–18 |

5 Fill in the missing letters to spell words and complete the sentences below.

Musi ____ m ____ k ____ s you sm ____ rt ____ r. Studi ____ s h ____ v ____ shown

th ____ t thos ____ who stu ____ y musi ____ ____ o b ____ tt ____ r in m ____ th and

s ____ i ____ n ____ ____. Musi ____ h ____ lps or ____ ____ niz ____ ____ n ____

____ ____ v ____ lop ____ hil ____ r ____ n's ____ r ____ ins. Musi ____ m ____ kin ____ ____ lso

m ____ k ____ s th ____ ____ l ____ ____ rly h ____ ____ lthi ____ r.

| 1–48 |

| 100 |

Unit 2 ACTIVITY 1 Name/Class_____

Counting Beats in $\frac{4}{4}$ Time

Place an "X" through each measure showing an incorrect number of beats in $\frac{4}{4}$ time.

10–100

Copyright © MM by Alfred Publishing Co., Inc.

Unit 2 ACTIVITY 2 Name/Class_____

Recognizing Repeated Measures

Circle the two measures in each staff that are identical.

10

Unit 2 **ACTIVITY 3**   Name/Class_____

Musical Math   Add and subtract the note values in $\frac{4}{4}$ time to get the total number of beats

1   𝅗𝅥 + 𝅗𝅥 − 𝅘𝅥 + 𝅝 = _____ beats

2   𝅝 − 𝅗𝅥 + 𝄽 + 𝅗𝅥 = _____ beats

3   𝅘𝅥 + 𝅘𝅥 + 𝅝 − 𝅛 = _____ beats

4   𝅝 + 𝅛 − 𝅗𝅥 − 𝅘𝅥 = _____ beats

5   𝅗𝅥 − 𝄽 + 𝅝 + 𝅗𝅥 = _____ beats

6   𝅘𝅥 + 𝅛 + 𝅗𝅥 − 𝄽 = _____ beats

7   𝅝 − 𝅘𝅥 + 𝅝 + 𝅗𝅥 = _____ beats

8   𝅗𝅥 + 𝅘𝅥 + 𝅛 + 𝅝 = _____ beats

9   𝅛 + 𝅝 + 𝅘𝅥 − 𝅘𝅥 = _____ beats

10   𝄽 + 𝅗𝅥 − 𝅛 + 𝅝 = _____ beats

10–100

11

Unit 2 ACTIVITY 4 Name/Class_____

Word Search

Find the words from the list below and circle them in the puzzle.
Words may appear forward, backward, up, down or diagonally, and may overlap.

T	I	M	E	S	I	G	N	A	T	U	R	E	O	H
N	V	D	T	T	S	S	C	M	S	S	J	W	G	E
U	O	C	O	D	O	U	B	L	E	B	A	R	F	E
Q	Y	T	N	Z	E	N	I	L	R	A	B	W	C	M
E	K	F	E	Q	A	Q	R	V	R	A	S	E	U	H
E	C	C	L	H	W	O	F	E	E	F	R	U	A	S
U	W	H	O	L	E	R	E	S	T	V	G	R	R	T
L	Y	A	H	U	Z	A	Z	Q	R	R	F	B	H	E
A	T	K	W	F	N	Z	D	J	A	C	A	S	Q	M
V	W	K	N	O	I	T	A	R	U	D	M	U	Y	P
E	M	U	K	X	R	S	O	J	Q	X	J	K	Q	O
T	W	N	S	E	T	O	N	F	L	A	H	N	P	Q
O	H	A	N	O	X	H	A	L	F	R	E	S	T	D
N	R	H	Y	T	H	M	J	W	P	H	I	J	U	O

Bar

Bar line

Beat

Count-off

Double bar

Duration

Half note

Half rest

Hanukkah

Measure

Notehead

Note value

Quarter note

Quarter rest

Rhythm

Stem

Tempo

Time signature

Whole note

Whole rest

5–100

12

Unit 2 **ACTIVITY 5** Name/Class_____

Music Crossword Puzzle

ACROSS

2. Lines that extend the lower and upper ranges of a staff (2 words)
5. Rest that receives 1 beat of silence in $\frac{4}{4}$ time (2 words)
8. Symbol for a musical silence
9. The length of a note
10. Two stacked numbers appearing after a clef sign (2 words)
14. One whole rest = _____ half rests.
16. Rest that receives 4 beats of silence in $\frac{4}{4}$ time (2 words)
17. Another name for measure
18. Rest that receives 2 beats of silence in $\frac{4}{4}$ time (2 words)
19. Line that divides music into equal sections (2 words)

DOWN

1. Note that receives 4 beats in $\frac{4}{4}$ time (2 words)
3. The bass and treble staffs connected by a brace and bar line (2 words)
4. Note that receives 1 beat in $\frac{4}{4}$ time (2 words)
6. The lines and spaces music is written on
7. ___ quarter rests = one whole rest
9. Lines at the end of a piece of music (2 words)
11. If a note appears on or above the 3rd line of the staff, the stem extends _____.
12. An introduction given before a piece of music that is performed to indicate the tempo
13. The area between bar lines
15. Note that receives 2 beats in $\frac{4}{4}$ time (2 words)

13

5–100

Unit 2 TEST Name/Class_____

1 ♩ is called a_____. In ⁴₄ time, it receives_____beat(s).

𝅝 is called a_____. In ⁴₄ time, it receives_____beat(s).

♩ is called a_____. In ⁴₄ time, it receives_____beat(s).

▬ is called a_____. In ⁴₄ time, rest for_____beat(s).

𝄾 is called a_____. In ⁴₄ time, rest for_____beat(s).

▬ is called a_____. In ⁴₄ time, rest for_____beat(s).

1–12	

2 Draw a bass clef and write the ⁴₄ time signature. Divide the entire staff line below into four equally spaced measures with a double bar at the end. Write four quarter notes on different pitches in each measure so that their stem direction alternates within the measure. Name the notes on the lines below the staff.

Clef, T-Sig. | 1–2

Bars | 2–8

Notes (each measure) | 2–8

___ ___ ___ ___   ___ ___ ___ ___   ___ ___ ___ ___   ___ ___ ___ ___

3 Add the following notes to get the total number of beats in ⁴₄ time.

𝅗𝅥 + ♩ + ♩ + ♩ + 𝅝 + ♩ + ♩ + ♩ + 𝅝 + 𝅝

2–10

4 Add the following rests to get the total number of beats in ⁴₄ time.

2–10

5 Draw a treble clef. Write the ⁴₄ time signature, and add bar lines and a double bar at the end. Write the beats below each measure, and the names of the notes above the staff.

London Bridge   **English Folk Song**

Clef, T-Sig. | 1–2

Bars | 1–8

Notes (each measure) | 1–8

Beats (each measure) | 1–8

6 Fill in the missing beats by adding only one note on the 2nd space in each measure. Write the beats under each measure.

3–12

7 Fill in the missing beats by adding only one rest to each measure. Write the beats under each measure.

3–12

100

14

Unit 3 ACTIVITY 1 Name/Class_____

Completing Measures in $\frac{2}{4}$, $\frac{3}{4}$ and $\frac{4}{4}$ Time

Professor Steinway is playing a concert tonight. Help her by completing
the measures below using either one note (N) or rest (R) as indicated.

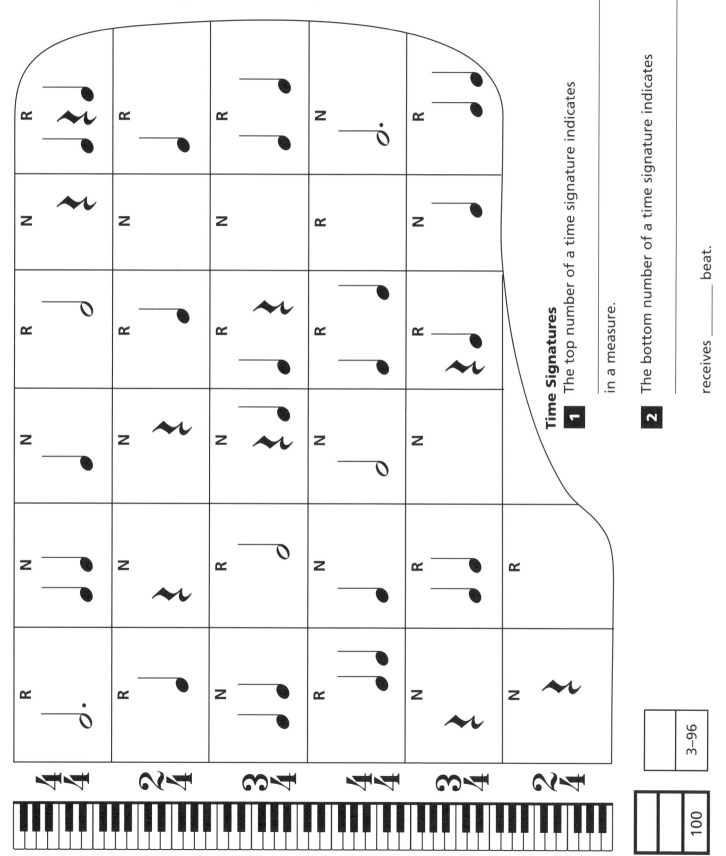

Time Signatures

1 The top number of a time signature indicates _____ in a measure.

2 The bottom number of a time signature indicates _____ receives _____ beat.

Identifying Time Signatures

Write the appropriate $\frac{2}{4}$, $\frac{3}{4}$ or $\frac{4}{4}$ time signature at the beginning of each line.

1 ____

2 ____

3 ____

4 ____

5 ____

Circle the measure with the incorrect number of beats in each example.

6 $\frac{2}{4}$

7 $\frac{3}{4}$

8 $\frac{3}{4}$

9 $\frac{2}{4}$

10 $\frac{4}{4}$

10–100

16

Unit 3 ACTIVITY 3 Name/Class_____

Writing Slurs and Ties

Add time signatures, then draw either a slur or tie to connect the bracketed notes in each example.
Label them "S" or "T."

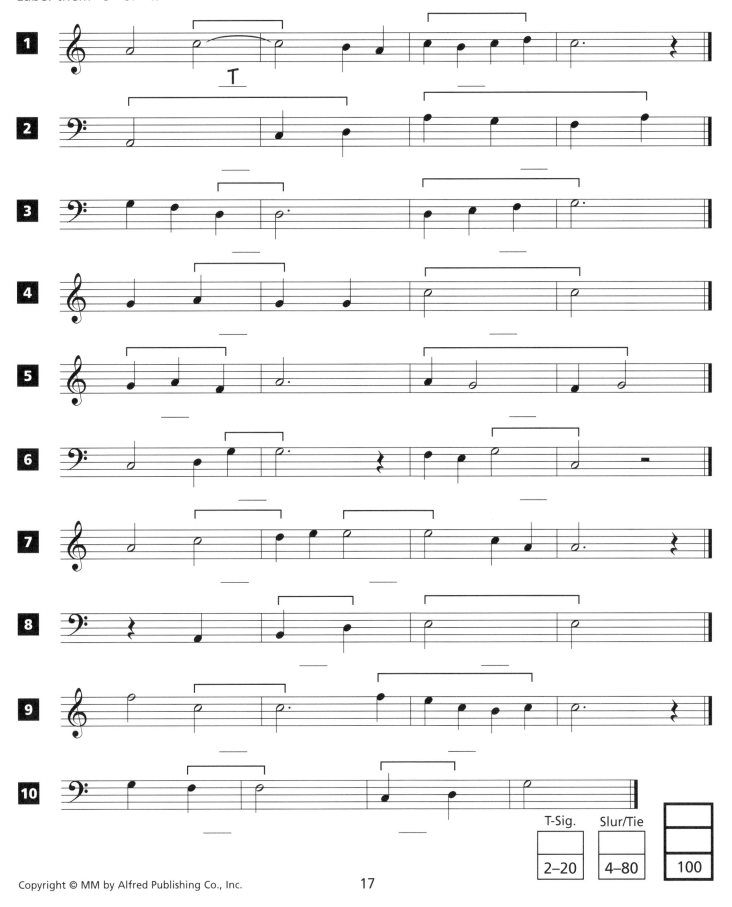

T-Sig.	Slur/Tie	
2–20	4–80	100

Unit 3 **ACTIVITY 4**   Name/Class_____

Musical Math

1   Add or subtract the notes as indicated and draw a note with the resulting value in the space.

a. $\frac{4}{4}$ 𝅗𝅥 · + ♩ = 𝅝   b. $\frac{3}{4}$ ♩ + ♩ = ___   c. $\frac{3}{4}$ 𝅗𝅥 − ♩ = ___

d. $\frac{4}{4}$ ♩ + 𝅗𝅥 = ___   e. $\frac{4}{4}$ 𝅝 − 𝅗𝅥· = ___   f. $\frac{2}{4}$ ♩ + ♩ = ___ | |
| 3–18 |

2   Write the total number of beats in each example.

a. ♩___𝅗𝅥· = ___   b. 𝅗𝅥___𝅗𝅥 = ___   c. 𝅗𝅥·___𝅗𝅥 = ___

d. 𝅝___♩ = ___   e. 𝅗𝅥___♩ = ___   f. 𝅝___𝅗𝅥· = ___ | |
| 3–18 |

3   Draw the bar lines in the following examples.

a.

b.

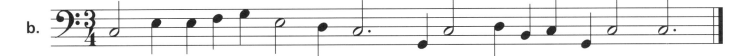

c. | |
| 7–21 |

4   Draw a treble clef, write a $\frac{4}{4}$ time signature and then add bar lines and a double bar at the end. Write the beats below each measure of the staff and the note names above the staff.

Hot Cross Buns

English Folk Song

Clef	T-Sig.	Bars	Notes	Beats (each measure)
5	5	1–8	1–17	1–8

| |
| |
| 100 |

Unit 3 ACTIVITY 5 Name/Class_____

Music Crossword Puzzle

ACROSS

1. A _____ rest is used for a full measure of rest.
4. On _____ instruments, a slur indicates a group of notes to be played in one bow.
7. Albert von Tilzer composed the song "Take Me Out to the_____ _____."
11. In ¾ time, two tied dotted half notes equal _____ beats.
13. A curved line that joins two notes of the same pitch
14. In ¾ and ⁴⁄₄ time, this note receives 3 beats. (3 words)
16. A half note receives _____ beats in ¾ time.
17. The tie should always be written on the _____ side from the note stems.
18. When stem direction is mixed, the slur is written _____ the notes.
20. A curved line that smoothly connects two or more notes of different pitches

DOWN

2. Two quarter rests equal the value of one _____ rest.
3. To play or sing notes smoothly connected
5. ²⁄₄ and ¾ are referred to as _____ _____ .
6. "Aura Lee" is an _____ folk song.
8. In ²⁄₄ time, the _____ note receives 1 beat.
9. A whole rest receives _____ beats in ¾ time.
10. On _____ instruments, only the first note of a group of slurred notes should be tongued.
12. On _____ instruments, slurs indicate when to lift the hands.
15. If the quarter note receives 1 beat, then the bottom number of the time signature is _____.
19. In ²⁄₄ time, the maximum number of half notes in a bar is _____.

5–100

Unit 3 **TEST** Name/Class_____

1 What kind of rest would you use for a complete measure of rest in 2/4 or 3/4 time?_____

2 A dot after a note increases its duration by_____the original value.

3 A curved line joining two notes of the same pitch is a _____.

4 A curved line smoothly connecting two or more notes of different pitch is a_____.

Exercises
1–5

5 Slurs indicate a group of notes to be played in one bow on_____instruments.

8–40

6 **a.** Complete the measures by adding one note in each.

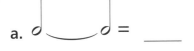

b. Complete the measures by adding one rest in each.

c. Complete the measures by adding one note or rest in each, as indicated.

Note   Rest   Note   Rest   Note   Rest   Note

2–30

7 Draw one note that equals the value of the tied notes.

a. 𝅗𝅥___𝅗𝅥 = _____   **b.** ♩___♩ = _____

c. 𝅗𝅥___♩ = _____   **d.** 𝅗𝅥·___♩ = _____

2–8

8 Add or subtract the rests as indicated, and draw one rest equal to the total number of beats.

a. 𝄽 + 𝄽 = ____   **b.** 𝄼 – 𝄽 = ____

c. 𝄼 + 𝄽 + 𝄽 = ____   **d.** 𝄼 – 𝄽 𝄽 = ____

3–12

9 Add a slur or tie in each example and label each with "S" or "T."

a.   b.   c.   d.   e.

____   ____   ____   ____   ____

2–10

100

Unit 4 ACTIVITY 1 Name/Class_____

Easy 8s: Adding Eighth Notes and Rests

To complete the measures below, add eighth notes, beamed or flagged, to the left "8," and eighth rests to the right "8."

Eighth Notes

Eighth Rests

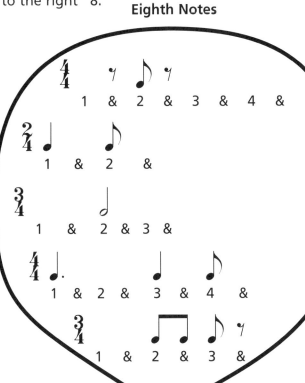

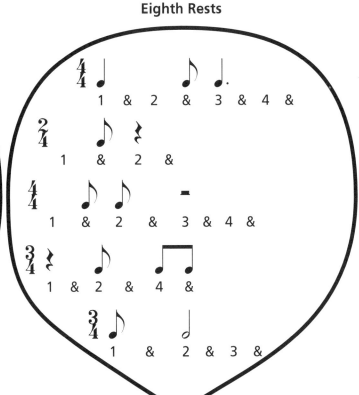

5–100

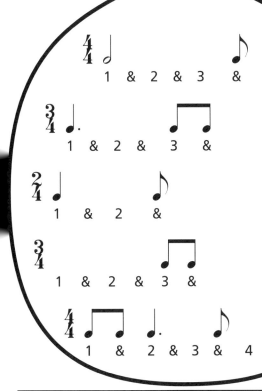

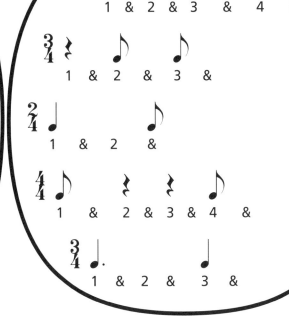

21

Unit 4 **ACTIVITY 2**   Name/Class_____

Word Scramble   Unscramble the letters to spell musical terms.

1 no hte ebta   _____ _____ _____ _____ ◯_____ _____ _____ _____

2 glfa   _____ ◯_____ _____ _____

3 dncsoe igednn   _____ ◯_____ _____ _____ _____ _____ _____ _____ _____ _____

4 hitehg srte   _____ _____ ◯_____ _____ _____

5 mbae   _____ _____ ◯_____ _____

6 hihetg toen   _____ ◯_____ _____ _____ _____ _____ _____

7 siftr inegnd   _____ _____ _____ _____ _____ ◯_____ _____ _____ _____

8 ptabeu   ◯_____ _____ - _____ _____ _____

9 aptere sgni   _____ _____ ◯_____ _____ _____ _____ _____

10 tedodt retuarq   _____ _____ _____ _____ _____ _____ ◯_____ _____

11 Write the words spelled by the circled letters above.

_____ _____ _____ _____   _____ _____ _____ _____ _____

Counting Eighth Notes and Eighth Rests
Write eighth notes to equal the value of the note given in each example.

12   𝅝 =

13   ♩ =

14   𝅗𝅥 =

15   ♩· =

16   𝅗𝅥· =

17   ♩ =

Write eighth rests to equal the value of the rest given in each example.

18   ▬ =   **19**   𝄽 =   **20**   ▬ =

22

5–100

Unit 4 **ACTIVITY 3** Name/Class_____

Repeat Signs, 1st and 2nd Endings

1 *Play It Again* Indicate the total number of beats, including repeats, in each example.

a. [music notation] ___   b. [music notation] ___

c. [music notation] ___   d. [music notation] ___

e. [music notation] ___   f. [music notation] ___

g. [music notation with 1st and 2nd endings] ___

h. [music notation with 1st and 2nd endings] ___

i. [music notation with 1st and 2nd endings] ___

2 *Tic Tac Toe*

Complete the measures with one note or rest as indicated.

Fill in the center square with the answer from column 1. Draw a vertical, horizontal or diagonal line through the notes and/or rests that add up to the time signature.

7–63

+1 if all correct

Column 1

a. [music notation] ___ Note

b. [music notation] ___ Rest

c. [music notation] ___ Note

Column 2

a.
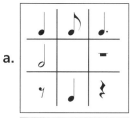

b.
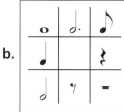

6–36

c.
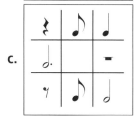

100

23

Unit 4 ACTIVITY 4 Name/Class_____

Word Search

Find the words from the list below and circle them in the puzzle.
Words may appear forward, backward, up, down or diagonally, and may overlap.

S	B	K	R	U	E	W	U	T	G	K	S	D	Q	R
G	U	E	G	N	I	D	N	E	D	N	O	C	E	S
Y	U	I	N	D	X	W	F	N	Z	T	U	T	T	O
Q	E	G	I	U	P	B	E	A	T	E	S	Z	O	Y
Z	X	H	D	N	I	V	C	E	B	O	A	L	N	H
W	V	T	N	L	O	R	D	X	F	L	A	G	H	T
J	H	H	E	H	E	Q	O	E	N	H	I	P	T	A
C	V	R	T	C	U	D	X	C	F	S	S	J	H	E
T	K	E	S	A	M	H	N	L	T	L	K	N	G	B
M	E	S	R	B	X	I	Z	A	U	W	J	B	I	E
B	Z	T	I	D	T	H	E	R	H	K	Y	W	E	H
L	E	Z	F	E	I	P	A	K	E	O	Q	W	D	T
R	Y	A	B	U	E	T	T	E	U	O	L	A	V	N
B	Q	P	M	R	C	Q	V	W	X	F	P	W	J	O

Alouette	Eighth note	Second ending
Bach	Eighth rest	Slur
Beam	First ending	Sousa
Beethoven	Flag	Tie
Clarke	Foster	Up-beat
Dotted quarter	Handel	Verdi
	On the beat	
	Repeat sign	

5–100

Use after completing page 26.

Music Crossword Puzzle

5–100

ACROSS

1. "Anvil Chorus" (from *Il Trovatore*) was composed by Giuseppe ____.
4. The composer of "Camptown Races" is Stephen ____ .
8. This note receives one-half beat in time signatures with 4 as the bottom number. (2 words)
10. "All Through the Night" is a ____ folk song.
12. A repeat sign means to either go back to the ____ or first repeat sign.
14. A dot after a note increases its duration by ____ the original value.
16. Four quarter rests equal one ____ rest.
18. Two eighth rests equal one ____ rest.
19. A note or rest on the "&" is considered an __.
20. This is what you add to a quarter note to change it into an eighth note.

DOWN

2. This rest receives one-half beat of silence in time signatures with 4 as the bottom number. (2 words)
3. The note that receives one and one-half beats in $\frac{2}{4}$, $\frac{3}{4}$ and $\frac{4}{4}$ time is a ____ ____ note.
5. Notes or rests on beats 1, 2, 3 and 4 are considered ___ ___ ___.
6. Two dots placed before a double bar (2 words)
7. Another way of indicating a repeat is with 1st and 2nd ____ .
9. "Hallelujah Chorus" (from *Messiah*) was composed by George Frideric ____.
11. A dotted quarter note is usually followed by an ____ note.
13. *Trumpet Voluntary* was composed by Jeremiah ____ .
15. *El Capitan* was composed by John Philip ____ .
17. In $\frac{2}{4}$, $\frac{3}{4}$ and $\frac{4}{4}$ time, the strongest beat is on beat number ____ .

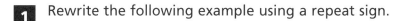 **Unit 4 TEST** Name/Class_____

1 Rewrite the following example using a repeat sign.

3–12

2 Rewrite the following example using 1st and 2nd endings.

Stodola Pumpa   **Czech Folk Song**

3–15

3 Add stems with flags or beams to make eighth notes as indicated.

One set of four   **Flags**   **Two sets of pairs**   **Flags**

3–12

4 Fill in the correct numbers to complete the answers.

a. ____ ♪ = 𝅗𝅥   b. ____ ♪ = ♩   c. ____ ♪ = o   d. ____ ♪ = 𝅗𝅥.

2–8

5 Complete the measure below using beamed eighth notes on the first space.
Write the beats (1&2&3&) under the notes.

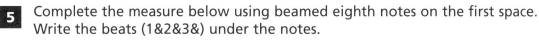

1–15

6 Fill in the correct numbers to complete the answers.

(⁴⁄₄ time)

a. ____ 𝄾 = 𝄽   b. ____ 𝄾 = 𝄽 + ▬   c. ____ 𝄾 = ▬   d. ____ 𝄾 = ▬

2–8

7 Complete the measures by adding only one rest to each,
as indicated by the arrows.

3–12

8 Complete the measures by adding only one note on the 4th line to each,
as indicated by the arrows.

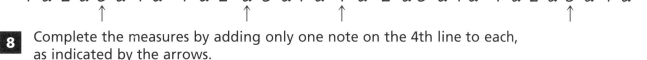

3–18

100

Unit 5 **ACTIVITY 1** Name/Class_____

Dynamic Signs

1 Write the Italian word and musical sign for each of the following English definitions.

Italian	Sign	English
		Very loud
		Moderately soft
		Soft
		Moderately loud
		Very soft
		Loud

5–30

2 Arrange the dynamic signs above in order from loudest to softest.

_____ _____ _____ _____ _____ _____

5–30

3 Write the Italian word and musical sign for each of the following English definitions.

Italian	Sign	English
		Gradually louder
		Gradually softer

5–10

4 Name two things that might have the dynamic marking of *piano*: (Example: leaves moving in a breeze)

a.

b.

5 Name two things that might have the dynamic marking of *forte*: (Example: a roaring lion)

a.

b.

5–10

5–10

6 What nationality of composers was among the first to use dynamic signs in their manuscripts?

_____

10

100

27

Unit 5 **ACTIVITY 2** Name/Class_____

Tempo Marks on Safari

1 On each line, write the Italian translation of the tempo mark indicated below the line. Use the following tempo marks:

Accelerando, Adagio, Allegro, Andante, Largo, Moderato, Ritardando, Vivace

In deepest Africa a jeep moves at a_____pace. Through the trees, a giraffe moves
moderate

at _____. A bird flies past the adventurers_____. Turning, they
walking speed   *quickly and cheerfully*

spot an elephant herd lumbering_____ toward them. Later, the passengers
slowly

of the jeep are startled when a lion runs past, _____. A hippo and her
lively and fast

baby move _____across the road and the jeep _____to a stop.
very slowly   *gradually slows*

As the sun sets over the plain, the jeep goes _____ , headed back to camp.
gradually faster

8–64

2 Number the pictures below from 1 (slowest) to 6 (fastest) and write the appropriate tempo marking for each on the line.

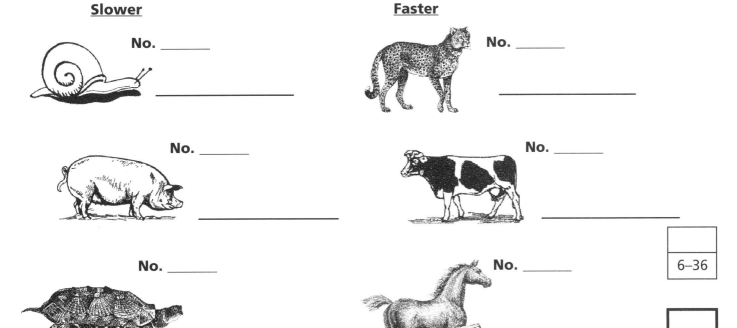

Slower   **Faster**

No. _____   No. _____

_____   _____

No. _____   No. _____

_____   _____

No. _____   No. _____

_____   _____

6–36

100

28

Unit 5 ACTIVITY 3 Name/Class_____

Matching Draw lines matching the terms on the left with their definitions on the right.

1 Tempo Marks and Dynamic Signs

Accelerando	Gradually softer
Adagio	Moving along (walking speed)
Allegro	Lively and fast
Andante	Gradually slower
Crescendo	Gradually faster
Diminuendo	Moderately
Largo	Gradually louder
Moderato	Very slow
Ritardando	Quickly, cheerfully
Vivace	Slow

5–50

Matching

2 Other Musical Terms

Accent	Hold the note for its full value
Coda	Rate of speed—how fast or slow the music is to be played
Da Capo	An added ending
Dal Segno	Hold the note longer than its normal value (approximately twice the normal duration)
Fermata	Play the note short and detached
Fine	A sudden, strong accent
Sforzando	The end
Staccato	Repeat from the beginning
Tempo	Repeat from the sign
Tenuto	Play the note louder, with a special emphasis

5–50

100

Unit 5 **ACTIVITY 4** Name/Class_____

Word Search

Find the words from the list below and circle them in the puzzle.
Words may appear forward, backward, up, down or diagonally, and may overlap.

I	Z	J	L	O	Z	Z	E	M	H	A	S	Y	X
O	F	X	T	E	N	U	T	O	C	L	F	Y	F
T	M	X	C	N	P	G	N	C	O	N	O	R	A
A	D	I	M	I	N	U	E	N	D	O	R	I	C
C	C	H	S	F	Q	L	C	S	A	G	Z	L	J
C	A	H	U	S	E	I	C	I	L	R	A	R	A
A	O	T	Q	R	I	T	A	R	D	A	N	D	O
T	C	I	A	E	A	T	E	Q	K	L	D	Q	I
S	F	N	G	M	B	T	R	W	D	U	O	V	R
P	D	O	T	A	R	E	D	O	M	M	P	J	I
O	A	T	G	O	D	E	P	N	F	K	R	U	I
X	Y	I	F	B	G	A	F	A	Y	J	K	Q	U
F	A	C	G	E	C	A	V	I	V	C	K	Q	T
W	I	N	X	A	P	C	J	P	I	M	H	C	L
G	H	B	D	N	O	Q	K	X	L	D	Q	V	F

Accelerando	Fermata	Piano
Accent	Fine	Ritardando
Adagio	Forte	Sforzando
Coda	Fortissimo	Staccato
Da Capo	Largo	Tenuto
Dal Segno	Mezzo	Vivace
Diminuendo	Moderato	

5–100

Unit 5 **ACTIVITY 5** Name/Class_____

Music Crossword Puzzle

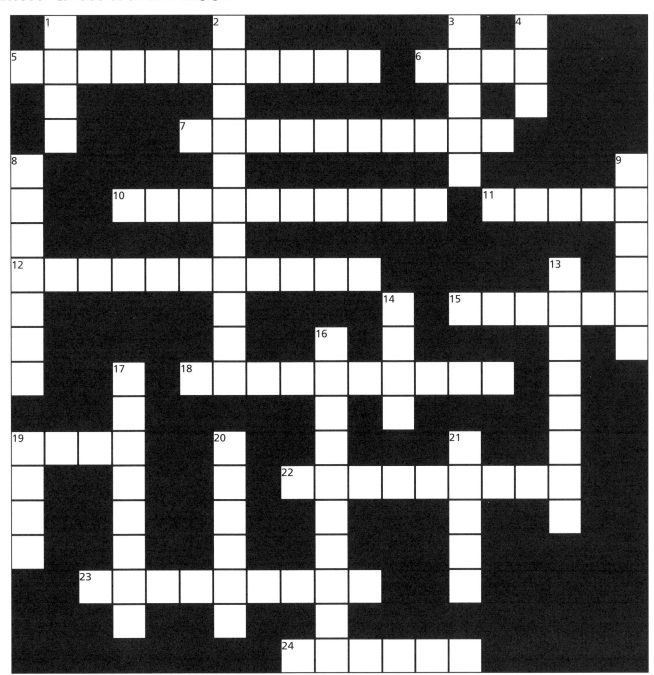

ACROSS

5. The Italian word for the ⟋ sign is ____ .
6. *Dal Segno* (D.S.) means repeat from the ____ .
7. The Italian words for *mp* are ____ ____ .
10. *Moderato* means ____ .
11. The Italian word for *f* is ____ .
12. The English translation of *Andante* is ____ ____ .
15. The symbol below the ♩ note to the right is an ____ .
18. The Italian word for *ff* is ____ .
19. *Mezzo piano* means moderately ____ .
22. The Italian word for the ⟍ sign is ____ .
23. *Da Capo* (D.C.) means repeat from the ____ .
24. *Rondo Alla Turca* was composed by Wolfgang Amadeus ____ .

DOWN

1. *issimo* means ____ .
2. The Italian word for gradually faster is ____ .
3. The Italian word for *p* is ____ .
4. *Fine* means the ____ .
8. The sign that means to hold a note longer than its normal value is a ____ .
9. The sign that means to hold a note for its full value is a ____ .
13. The English translation of *Largo* is ____ ____ .
14. The English translation of *Vivace* is lively and ____ .
16. The Italian word for gradually slower is ____ .
17. *Staccato* means to play the note short and ____ .
19. The English translation of *Adagio* is ____ .
20. A *Coda* (✛) is an added ____ .
21. The Italian word that tells how fast or slow to play the music is ____ .

4–100

Unit 5 TEST Name/Class_____

1 Write the dynamic sign for each of the following Italian words.

a. piano_____   **b.** pianissimo _____   **c.** decrescendo_____

d. forte _____   **e.** fortissimo _____   **f.** mezzo piano _____

g. mezzo forte_____   **h.** crescendo_____

2–16

2 Write the English definitions of the following tempo marks.

a. Moderato _____   **b.** Allegro _____

c. Accelerando _____   **d.** Largo _____

e. Vivace _____   **f.** Ritardando _____

g. Adagio _____   **h.** Andante _____

2–16

3 Draw a quarter note with the stem down utilizing the following articulations.

5–20

a. Staccato: **b.** Tenuto: **c.** Accent: **d.** Fermata:

4 Write the symbol for sforzando. _____

8

5 Write out the following musical example as it would actually be played without using **D.S. al Fine** or **Fine**.

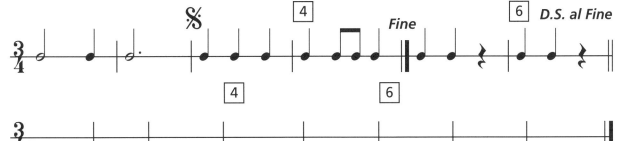

2–16

6 Write out the following musical example as it would actually be played without using **D.S. al Coda** or ⊕ **Coda**.

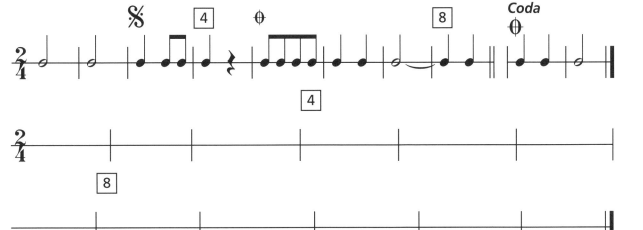

2–24

100

Unit 6 **ACTIVITY 1** Name/Class_____

Sharps, Flats and Natural Signs

| | 5 |

1 A sharp sign (circle one)   **raises**   **lowers**   the pitch of a note.

| | 5 |

2 A flat sign (circle one)   **raises**   **lowers**   the pitch of a note.

3 Place a sharp sign to the left of each note, then write the note names on the corresponding piano keys.

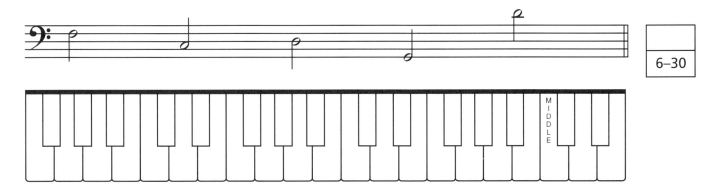

| | 6–30 |

4 Place a flat sign to the left of each note, then write the note names on the corresponding piano keys.

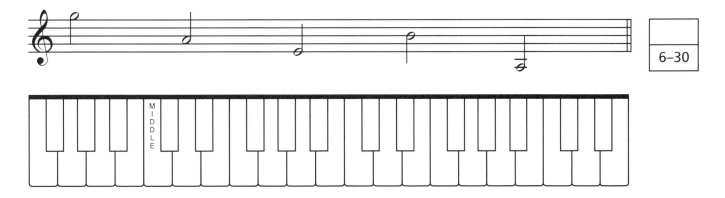

| | 6–30 |

5 Place a natural sign to the left of each repeated note, then write the note names on the corresponding piano keys.

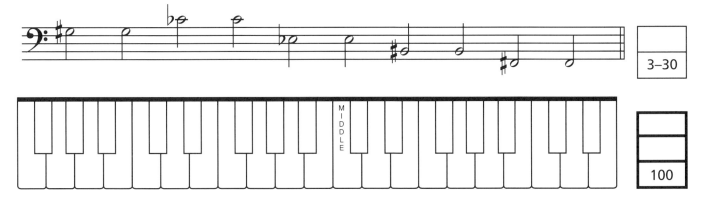

| | 3–30 |

| | 100 |

33

Unit 6 **ACTIVITY 2** Name/Class_____

Whole Steps and Half Steps

1 Write the note that is one half step *above* each given note,
using ♯ and ♮ signs as appropriate.

3–18

Example

2 Write the note that is one half step *below* each given note,
using ♭ and ♮ signs as appropriate.

3–18

3 Write the note that is one whole step *above* each given note,
using ♯ and ♮ signs as appropriate.

3–18

4 Write the note that is one whole step *below* each given note,
using ♭, ♯ and ♮ signs as appropriate.

3–18

5 Indicate whether each pair of notes is a half or whole step apart by
writing "H" or "W" in the space provided.

4–28

100

34

Enharmonic Notes

1 Draw the note that is the enharmonic equivalent to the note in each measure.

3–39

2 Rewrite the following measures using enharmonic notes.

3–24   +1 Clef, T-Sig.

3 Draw a line matching each note with its enharmonic equivalent.

2–36

a. **Sharps to Flats**		b. **Flats to Sharps**	
C♯	E♭	G♭	B♯
F♯	F♭	C	E♯
E	D♭	D♭	D♯
D♯	A♭	B♭	C♯
B	B♭	E♭	B
G♯	C♭	F	A♯
B♯	G♭	A♭	F♯
A♯	F	F♭	G♯
E♯	C	C♭	E

100

Unit 6 ACTIVITY 4 Name/Class_____

Word Search

Find the words from the list below and circle them in the puzzle.
Words may appear forward, backward, up, down or diagonally, and may overlap.

A	A	Z	N	G	I	S	P	R	A	H	S	A	E
H	S	L	A	T	N	E	D	I	C	C	A	N	M
J	Y	J	T	G	W	A	J	C	Z	R	H	I	N
K	K	H	U	P	E	T	S	F	L	A	H	G	D
H	S	M	R	L	M	Q	D	F	R	M	I	M	G
A	V	R	A	P	I	V	L	M	I	S	I	G	C
W	O	F	L	R	Y	U	O	Q	T	U	L	M	I
H	K	Z	S	W	C	N	S	A	H	C	R	P	H
O	I	H	I	O	I	H	L	F	N	R	R	U	V
L	A	V	G	C	G	F	S	O	U	I	T	A	D
E	H	C	N	Q	Z	Q	C	L	V	C	W	R	E
S	C	O	M	J	A	V	W	H	A	F	I	G	J
T	T	N	D	D	W	R	U	V	S	V	I	K	O
E	X	P	F	W	Z	L	G	O	N	D	D	E	O
P	V	X	K	M	C	V	S	G	M	E	D	Q	V

Accidentals	Half step	Sharp sign
Circus March	Julius Fucik	Tchaikovsky
Enharmonic note	March Slav	Whole step
Flat sign	Natural sign	

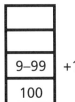

9–99 +1 if all correct
100

Music Crossword Puzzle

ACROSS

1. On the keyboard, a note appearing after a natural sign is always a ____ key.
8. ♮ is known as a ____ sign.
9. Julius Fučik is the composer of ____ ____, from *Entry of the Gladiators*.
10. When you flat a note on the keyboard, you play the next key to the ____ .
11. A sharp sign before a note ____ the pitch of that note.
14. ♯ is known as a ____ sign.
15. A natural sign before a note ____ a previous sharp or flat.

DOWN

1. The distance from any key on the keyboard to two keys above or below, is a ____ ____ .
2. When you sharp a note on the keyboard, you play the next key to the ____ .
3. A flat sign before a note ____ the pitch of that note.
4. When ♭, ♯ or ♮ signs appear within a musical piece, they are called ____ .
5. *March Slav* was composed by Peter Ilyich ____ .
6. Notes that sound the same but are written differently are called ____ notes.
7. ♭ is known as a ____ sign.
12. The distance from any key on the keyboard to the very next key above or below is a ____ ____ .
13. The number of measures an accidental is in effect is ____ .

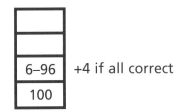

6–96   +4 if all correct
100

37

Unit 6 TEST   Name/Class_____

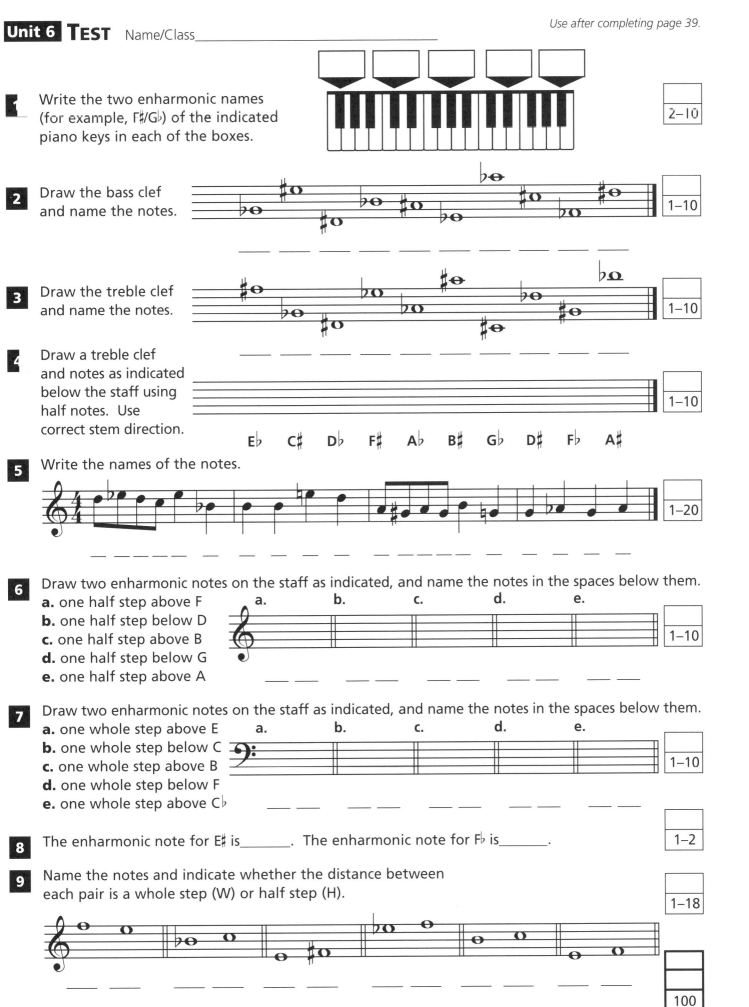

1 Write the two enharmonic names (for example, F♯/G♭) of the indicated piano keys in each of the boxes.

2–10

2 Draw the bass clef and name the notes.

1–10

3 Draw the treble clef and name the notes.

1–10

4 Draw a treble clef and notes as indicated below the staff using half notes. Use correct stem direction.

1–10

E♭   C♯   D♭   F♯   A♭   B♯   G♭   D♯   F♭   A♯

5 Write the names of the notes.

1–20

6 Draw two enharmonic notes on the staff as indicated, and name the notes in the spaces below them.
a. one half step above F
b. one half step below D
c. one half step above B
d. one half step below G
e. one half step above A

a.   b.   c.   d.   e.

1–10

7 Draw two enharmonic notes on the staff as indicated, and name the notes in the spaces below them.
a. one whole step above E
b. one whole step below C
c. one whole step above B
d. one whole step below F
e. one whole step above C♭

a.   b.   c.   d.   e.

1–10

8 The enharmonic note for E♯ is_____. The enharmonic note for F♭ is_____.

1–2

9 Name the notes and indicate whether the distance between each pair is a whole step (W) or half step (H).

1–18

100

Copyright © MM by Alfred Publishing Co., Inc.   38

Student Name

Book 1

	Unit ___						Unit ___						Unit ___					
	1	2	3	4	5	T	1	2	3	4	5	T	1	2	3	4	5	T